A Salute to Black Scientists and Inventors

Copyright © 1985, 1996 by Empak Publishing Company

ISBN 0-922162-2-6 (Volume II)
ISBN 0-922162-15-8 (Volume Set)

A Salute to Black Scientists and Inventors

EMPAK PUBLISHING COMPANY

Publisher & Editor: Richard L. Green
Assoc. Editor: Dorothy M. Love-Carroll, Kathy Reid
Researcher: Dorothy M. Love-Carroll, Mell Weatherly
Production: Dickinson & Associates, Inc.
Illustration: S. Gaston Dobson
Foreword: Robert C. Hayden

"... the color of the skin is in no way connected with strength of the mind or intellectual powers...."

Benjamin Banneker
1796

On behalf of Empak Publishing Company, I am pleased to endorse the second in a special series of Black History publications: *"A Salute to Black Scientists and Inventors,"* produced by Empak. This booklet gives recognition to eighteen Black Americans who made significant contributions to science and technology in America during the 19th and 20th centuries.

"A Salute to Black Scientists and Inventors" is an enlightening commentary on the ingenuity of eighteen extraordinary innovators whose genius shone through the roadblocks of adversity and racial barriers to provide mankind something called convenience, quality of life, luxury and even order. They industrialized the burden of labor and created new ways to ease the plight of servitude and affliction.

The modernization of machinery that we casually accept as a given was once a nonexistent commodity were it not for the contributions of these gifted men. The remedies and treatments now commonly employed in hospitals and clinics would be a mystery if not for the brilliance of these men. These scientists and inventors were anachronisms, many years ahead of their contemporaries in terms of thought and adventure, yet they faced the challenges of trial and error, financial responsibility and rejection with perseverance and dedication.

Over the years the lives of these great scientists and inventors depicted in this publication have been an inspiration to me. The impact of these unsung heroes should be especially inspiring to our youth, who aspire to achieve exceptional goals, particularly in the field of science and engineering. *"A Salute to Black Scientists and Inventors"* is an educational asset that any individual or organization will find beneficial.

When all Americans, young and old, Black and White, come to know these individuals, we will all have a greater understanding and respect for these prolific men, their genius and their contributions. Major industries in present-day America and abroad are the direct benefactors of the endeavors of the

Black inventor and scientist. A creative, inventive mind knows no racial limitation or boundary.

I congratulate and commend Empak Publishing Company for affording you and me the opportunity to learn and reacquaint ourselves with these American scientists and inventors in *"A Salute to Black Scientists and Inventors."*

Robert C. Hayden

EDITOR'S NOTE: In his own right, Robert C. Hayden, educator, Black historian and author has also made significant contributions to Black America. He is the Executive Assistant to the Superintendent of the Boston Public Schools; Executive Council Member, National Association for the Study of Afro-American Life and History; Lecturer in African-American Studies, Northeastern University in Boston.

CONTENTS

Editor's Note: Due to this booklet's space limitations, some facts on the lives of the above noted Black Scientists and Inventors have been omitted.

BENJAMIN BANNEKER
1731-1806

Benjamin Banneker was a self-taught mathematician, outstanding astronomer, author of almanacs, renown surveyor, humanitarian, and celebrated inventor.

Benjamin Banneker was born near Baltimore, Maryland, in 1731. He was the only child of a free mulatto mother and African father, who purchased his own freedom from slavery. Banneker lived all of his life on his parents' farm on the Patapsco River in Baltimore County. Young Benjamin attended integrated private schools, and obtained an eighth grade education by age 15, and excelled in mathematics. He took over his parents' farm and became an excellent farmer.

Josef Levi, a traveling salesman, showed Banneker a pocket watch, something he had never seen before. He became so fascinated over the watch that Levi gave it to him. He took the watch home and spent days taking it apart and putting it back together. In 1753, using the watch as a model, Banneker produced the first wooden clock ever built in the United States. It was made entirely of wood, and each gear was carved by hand. His clock kept perfect time, striking every hour, for more than forty years. News of the clock created such a sensation that people came from all over to see it, and the genius who made it.

During the revolutionary war period, George Ellicot, a neighbor, introduced Banneker to the science of astronomy, which he rapidly mastered. His aptitude in mathematics and knowledge of astronomy enabled him to predict the solar eclipse that took place on April 14, 1789. In 1792, Banneker began publishing an almanac that was widely read and became the main reference for farmers in the Mid-Atlantic states. It offered weather data, recipes, medical remedies, poems and anti-slavery essays. This almanac was the first scientific book written by a Black American, and it was published annually for more than a decade.

Banneker's major reputation stems from his service as a surveyor on the six-man team which helped design the blueprints for Washington, D.C. President Washington had appointed Banneker, making him the first Black presidential appointee in the United States. Banneker helped in selecting the sites for the U.S. Capitol building, the U.S. Treasury building, the White House and other Federal buildings. When the chairman of the civil engineering team, Major L'Enfant, abruptly resigned and returned to France with the plans, Banneker's photographic memory enabled him to reproduce them in their entirety. Washington, D.C., with its grand avenues and buildings, was completed and stands today as a monument to Banneker's genius.

Banneker's preoccupation with scientific matters in no way diminished his concern for the plight of Blacks. In a twelve-page letter to Thomas Jefferson, he refuted the statement that "Blacks were inferior to Whites." Jefferson changed his position and, as a testimonial, sent a copy of Banneker's almanac to the French Academy of Sciences in Paris. Another was used in Britain's House of Commons to support an argument for the education of Blacks. Banneker was living proof that "the strength of mind is in no way connected with the color of the skin."

Banneker's predictions were consistently accurate, except for his prediction of his own death. Living four years longer than he had predicted, Banneker died on October 25, 1806, wrapped in a blanket observing the stars through his telescope.

ANDREW JACKSON BEARD
1849-c. 1921

Andrew Jackson Beard invented the Automatic Railroad Car Coupler, commonly referred to as the "Jenny" Coupler. Railroad car coupling is an automatic process for hooking railroad cars together.

Andrew Beard was born a slave in Jefferson County, Alabama, in 1849. He was emancipated at the age of 15, and married at 16.

Beard was a farmer near Birmingham, Alabama for some five years, but recalled visiting Montgomery in 1872, with 50 bushels of apples drawn by oxen. He said, "It took me three weeks to make the trip. I quit farming after that." Instead, he built and operated a flour mill in Hardwicks, Alabama. He began pondering the mechanics of his plow invention.

Beard's idea flourished and, in 1881, he patented one of his plows and sold it, in 1884, for $4,000. On December 15, 1887, Beard invented another plow and sold it for $5,200. With these profits, he went into the real estate business and accumulated a profit of about $30,000.

In 1889, Beard invented a rotary steam engine, patented on July 5, 1892. He claimed that his steam engine was cheaper to build and operate than conventional steam engines and it would not explode. While Beard worked on his rotary steam engine, he experimented with the automatic car coupler idea. In the early days of American railroading, coupling was done manually.

While working in the railroad yards in Eastlake, Alabama, Beard developed an idea for a device which would automatically hook railroad cars together. Car coupling, an extremely dangerous procedure, required a railroad worker to brace himself between cars and drop a metal pin into place at the exact moment the rail cars came together. Few railroad men kept all their fingers, many lost arms and hands. And, many were caught between the rail cars and crushed to death during the hazardous split-second operation. Beard himself lost a leg as a result of a car coupling accident.

Beard's "Jenny" coupler automatically secured two rail cars by merely bumping them together. He filed his patent application in September, 1897 and the patent for his invention was issued two month later on November 23rd. He was later paid $50,000 for the rights of his patent by a New York manufacturing firm.

Andrew Beard's invention, which was improved in 1899, is a forerunner of today's automatic coupler. Unfortunately, his life, after 1897, is a virtual mystery; no record has been found of where he died. However, the railroad industry, both past and present, owes an enormous debt to Andrew Beard's inventive genius.

GEORGE WASHINGTON CARVER
1860-1943

George Washington Carver, a botanist and agricultural chemist, was undoubtedly one of the greatest scientists of all times. He revolutionized and revitalized the dying agricultural industry of the South between 1900 and 1930.

Carver was born of slave parents on Moses Carver's plantation, near Diamond Grove, Missouri, in 1860. Although Carver's early education was sketchy, at ten years of age, George struck out on his own to get a formal education. Ironically, when George showed up at a high school in Kansas, he was promptly told to leave as soon as the headmaster saw he was Black. Disillusioned, yet determined, he remained in Kansas working odd jobs as a farm hand, a cook and a laundry helper.

George was twenty-five years old when he started his freshman year at Simpson College in Iowa. In 1891, after two years at Simpson, he entered Iowa Agricultural College, now the Iowa State University at Ames, Iowa. While there, George did outstanding work in botany and agricultural chemistry. After graduating as one of Iowa's outstanding scholars, he remained at Iowa State to pursue another degree. Because of his outstanding work with plants and soil, Carver was made an assistant instructor in botany and appointed green house director.

Shortly after receiving his Master's Degree in 1896, Carver received a letter from Booker T. Washington, head of Tuskegee Institute, asking for his instructional help. Carver replied, "I am coming." He spent the remaining years of his life at Tuskegee as an agricultural scientist. While there, he gradually won the acceptance of the southern farmers, selling his idea of "plant rotation" to keep the soil enriched. The cotton plant had been grown in the South for nearly 200 years, depleting the soil's minerals. Carver told them to plant peanuts, clover and peas, since these crops would replenish the minerals as they grew, because the roots of these plants brought nitrogen to the soil.

In his lab at Tuskegee, Carver discovered over two dozen products, such as milk and cheese, that could be synthesized from the peanut. He eventually developed over 300 different products, including instant coffee, face cream, ink, shampoo and soaps made from the oils, proteins and chemicals of peanuts. Soon, new industries sprang up which made use of these peanut products, and the South began to prosper economically. He produced similar results with sweet potatoes, pecans and southern clay.

In 1916, Carver received an honor, given to few Americans, when elected a fellow of the Royal Society of Arts, Manufactures and Commerce of Great Britain. In subsequent years, he received many other distinguished honors.

Carver remained a bachelor, and he died on Tuskegee Institute's campus, January 5, 1943. He left his life's savings of $33,000 to establish the George Washington Carver Foundation, which helped to provide research opportunities for scientists. This foundation still thrives today.

George Washington Carver was held in high esteem the world over. As a testimony to Carver's distinguished career, a memorial was erected at Tuskegee in his honor, along with the founding of the George Washington Carver Museum. Approved by joint resolution of Congress, on December 28, 1945, George Washington Carver Day was proclaimed on January 5, 1946.

The farmland near Diamond Grove, Missouri, where Carver was born, is now a national landmark of the U.S. Government, paying homage to an ingenious chemist whose research and contributions benefitted all people throughout the world.

DR. CHARLES RICHARD DREW
1904-1950

Dr. Charles Richard Drew was a world renowned surgeon, medical scientist, educator and authority on the preservation of blood. He was the pioneer of blood plasma preservation, leaving mankind an important legacy, the blood bank.

Born in 1904, in Washington, D.C., he was the eldest of five children born to Charles and Nora Drew. He was an outstanding athlete. Graduating from Dunbar High School, in 1922, he excelled in football, basketball, swimming and track with much acclaim. At Amherst College in Massachusetts, he was an achiever in both sports and academics, graduating in 1926 with high honors. He went on to become an instructor of biology and chemistry, and Director of Athletics at Morgan State College in Baltimore, Maryland.

Charles Drew loved sports and was a tough competitor. He could have become a professional athlete or coach, but his desire to become a doctor was stronger. In 1928, Drew entered McGill University Medical School, in Montreal, Canada, and won membership in its Medical Honorary Society. It was at McGill that he became interested in blood research. He received his Master of Surgery and Doctor of Medicine degrees in 1933.

After internships at the Royal Victoria Hospital and the Montreal General Hospital, in Canada, he taught at Howard University's Medical School. Afterwards, at Columbia Presbyterian Hospital, in New York City, he researched a process for blood preservation. During his two years at Columbia, he developed a technique for the long-term preservation of blood plasma. He earned the Doctor of Science in Medicine degree in 1940, with a dissertation on "Banked Blood."

In World War II, England suffered heavy casualties and called upon Dr. Drew to initiate its military blood bank program. There he introduced preserved blood plasma on the battlefield. This system worked so well that the British asked him to organize the world's first mass blood bank project. Dr. Drew also became the first Director of the American Red Cross Blood Bank.

Also during the 1940s, Dr. Drew received scores of awards and honors, and was recognized as one of the world's leading physicians. In 1941, Dr. Drew resigned his position with the AMRC blood bank, after the War Department sent out a directive stating that blood taken from White donors should not be mixed with that of Black donors. This issue caused widespread controversy. Drew called the order a stupid blunder. He further stated that "the blood of individual human beings may differ by blood groupings, but there is absolutely no scientific basis to indicate any difference in human blood from race to race." He returned to Howard University to teach surgery at its medical school.

Dr. Drew was killed in an automobile accident while on a trip to a medical meeting at Tuskegee Institute in 1950. The irony of his death is that his life may have been saved, if he had received immediate medical attention following the accident. Discrimination at nearby White hospitals did not allow him the blood transfusions needed to save his life.

Every blood bank in the world is a living memorial to the genius of Dr. Charles Richard Drew. His name will live on forever in medical history. Schools and health clinics throughout the United States have been named in honor of Drew and his ingenious gift to mankind.

JAMES FORTEN, SR.
1766-1842

James Forten, Sr. invented and perfected a sail designed to make the guiding of ships easier. In addition to becoming a prosperous businessman in the sail making industry, he was an abolitionist, a champion of Blacks' rights, and a leader of reform movements long before the emergence of Frederick Douglass.

James Forten, Sr. was born in Philadelphia, in 1766, as a free Black. His parents, Thomas and Sarah Forten, were also born free; but his grandparents were brought to America as slaves from Africa. Forten's elementary school education began in the colored children's free school of Anthony Benezet, a renowned Quaker abolitionist.

At the age of eight, Forten began working in a Philadelphia sail loft with his father. The loft was owned by Robert Bridges. James later worked in a grocery store to help support his mother, after his father's death from a boating accident in 1775. His formal education ended at the age of ten.

At 14, Forten urged his mother to let him sign up on a ship, the *Royal Lewis,* as a powder boy during the Revolutionary War. He later returned home to begin a sailmaking apprenticeship in Mr. Bridges' sail loft. Bridges, who was now getting older, appointed young Forten foreman of his sail loft in 1786. When Bridges retired in 1798, he loaned Forten the money to buy his loft. At the age of 32, Forten had a work force of 38 men; 19 were White.

Due partly to Forten's innovative sailmaking, his sail loft became one of the most prosperous in Philadelphia. Two years later, he built a luxurious three-story home for his second wife, Charlotte, on Philadelphia's Lombard Street.

James Forten's abolitionist activities were numerous. His amassed fortune enabled him to buy many slaves' freedom (On one occasion, he bought a whole family's freedom). Congress' overwhelming rejection of a petition presented by the Free Blacks of Philadelphia (suggesting a modification of the *Fugi-*

tive Slave Act probably sparked Forten's decision to become an abolitionist.

Forten, along with Black leaders Richard Allen and Absalom Jones, enlisted the help of 2,500 Blacks to help guard Philadelphia against the British during the War of 1812. He also used his leadership to solicit many of the first 1,700 Black subscribers for William Lloyd Garrison's newspaper, The Liberator, and donated money to help cover the paper's first 27 subscriptions. His Lombard Street home served as an Underground Railroad way station for escaping slaves. These examples are only a few of the many activities that Forten was involved in, for he maintained a strong stance against colonization and slavery.

This inventor-businessman, James Forten, Sr., used his resources to improve the life for his people. He spent over half of his $300,000 fortune (a large sum at that time) to finance different crusades for abolitionists' activities. He was a forerunner for civil rights and a true humanitarian.

LLOYD AUGUSTUS HALL
1894-1971

Lloyd A. Hall, a pioneering industrial food chemist, revolutionized the meatpacking industry with his development of curing salts for the processing and preserving of meats. His patented chemical processes also benefitted other food products.

Hall was born in Elgin, Illinois on June 20, 1894. He was an honor student at the East Side High School in Aurora, Illinois, where he developed his interest in chemistry. He graduated among the top ten of his class of 125, and received four scholarships to attend outstanding universities. He selected Northwestern University, where he earned a degree in pharmaceutical chemistry. Afterwards, he pursued graduate degrees at the University of Chicago and the University of Illinois.

In 1916, his chemistry background enabled him to obtain a position as a chemist in the Chicago Department of Health laboratory. He was promoted to senior chemist within one year, and subsequently worked as a chief chemist at the John Morrell Company in Ottumwa, Iowa. Two years later, Hall's interests shifted to food chemistry. He was now chief chemist at the Boyer Griffith Laboratories. By 1922, he became president and chemical director of consulting at Griffith Laboratories. He relinquished his position as president to become chief chemist and director of research. He maintained this position for 37 years, until his retirement in 1959.

Before Hall's discovery, salts used for preserving and curing meat products were unsatisfactory. He prepared a new salt mixture of sodium nitrate and sodium nitrite. By "flash-drying" (evaporating) the solution, he formed preserving crystals far superior to any meat-curing salts ever produced.

Hall was also successful in new sterilization techniques for foods and spices. He used ethylene oxide gas in a vacuum chamber with foodstuffs, effectively sterilizing them and enhancing their appearance, quality and flavor. Hall's method of sterilization with ethylene oxide became big business in the United States, for hospital supplies such as bandages, dressing, dentirifices, cosmetics and other products.

During World War I, Hall was appointed chief inspector of powder and explosives in the U.S. Army. In World War II, he was invaluable in solving problems of maintaining military food supplies in pure and edible form. In 1951, he and an associate patented a process that significantly reduced the time for curing bacon.

Dr. Hall published over 50 scientific papers, and received 105 U.S. and foreign patents. He is listed in *American Men of Science, Who's Who in Chemistry, Who's Who in Colored America, and Who's Who in America.* Dr. Hall died in 1971, leaving a legacy of innovations in the food preservation industry.

FREDERICK McKINLEY JONES
1892-1961

Frederick McKinley Jones was the inventor of the first practical refrigeration system for longhaul trucks. His system was later adapted to a variety of other carriers including ships and railway cars.

A native of Cincinnati, Ohio, born in 1892, he was orphaned at the age of nine, never managing to get more than a sixth grade education. Jones moved to Covington, Kentucky where he was raised by a priest until the age of 16. When he left the rectory, Jones hitched rides in automobiles and became interested in how they worked. He returned to Cincinnati and finally convinced a garage owner to hire him as a mechanic. Jones became garage foreman of the automobile shop in three years.

By the age of 19, Jones had built several racing cars which he drove in racing exhibitions. His fervent desire to see his cars being raced prompted him to attend competitions without permission from his boss. For this, he was fired from his foreman position.

Jones later accepted a job as chief mechanic on a 30,000 acre farm in Hallock, Minnesota. He expanded his mechanical skills and knowledge through his library studies. Jones later served as an electrician in the United States Army, in France during World War I, achieving the rank of sergeant.

When the war was over, Jones returned to Hallock and entered a new area of electronic research. He built the first transmitter for the Hallock radio station and designed a "talking" movie projector. Although a typical commercial projector would cost about $3,000, Jones was able to build one from odds and ends for less than $100. When motion pictures incorporated soundtracks, Jones built his own device using creative ideas and information he had researched.

Hearing about Jones and his mechanical ability, Joseph A. Numero, owner of a motion picture equipment company, offered Jones a position as an electronic engineer. Sound equipment made by Numero's film was used in movie houses throughout the Midwest. In 1938, Jones received his first patent for a ticket dispensing machine used by movie houses.

By the late 1930s, Jones was busy designing portable air-cooling units for trucks that would preserve perishable foods transported to markets from one end of the country to the other. Numero formed a partnership with Jones as vice president. By 1949, the U.S. Thermo Control Company had grown to a $3,000,000 a year business, manufacturing refrigeration units for trains, ships and airplanes.

The crisis of World War II inspired Jones to design a special refrigeration unit that would keep blood serum fresh for transfusions and medicines. Jones was recognized as an authority in refrigeration engineering. In 1944, he was elected to membership in the American Society of Refrigeration Engineers. During the 1950s, he served as a consultant on refrigeration problems to both the U.S. Defense Department and Bureau of Standards.

Frederick McKinley Jones died in Minneapolis, Minnesota, in 1961, credited with more than 60 patents, 40 for refrigeration equipment alone. Jones' invention completely changed the food transport industry, creating international markets for food crops.

Percy Lavon Julian was a brilliant organic chemist, whoes many significant discoveries benefitted all of mankind. His dream was that one day the scientific world would be more receptive to the Black scientific mind.

Percy Julian was born in Montgomery, Alabama in 1899. His father was a railway mail clerk and his mother a school teacher. Julian attended the State Normal School for Negroes, a private high school in Montgomery. After graduating he entered DePauw University in Greencastle, Indiana. He was class valedictorian and a member of two honor societies, Phi Beta Kappa and Sigma Chi.

Julian taught at Fisk University before entering Harvard University, where he received a Master's Degree in chemistry. After accepting a teaching position at West Virginia College for Blacks, he transferred to Howard University in Washington, D.C., serving as associate professor of chemistry for two years. In 1929, with financial backing from the General Education Board, Julian went abroad to Vienna, to study for his Ph.D. While there, he became interested in the research of soybeans.

In 1931, Julian he received his Ph.D. in organic chemistry. Upon returning to DePauw, he and his assistant, Dr. Pikl, were the first to synthesize physostigmine, a drug used in the treatment of glaucoma. The Dean of the University wanted to appoint Julian as chairman of the chemistry department, but was advised against it because Julian was Black.

Julian left DePauw accepting employment at Glidden Company, a manufacturer of paints and varnishes. In 1936, he was appointed chief chemist and director of research of soybean products. His appointment was viewed as a turning point regarding the acceptance of Black scientists in America.

Dr. Julian saved the lives of thousands of servicemen in World War II with his invention of "aero-foam," derived from soybeans, which was used to extinguish fires. He also discovered a more economical way to extract sterols from soybean oil to produce sex hormones. Dr. Julian is probably best known for the development of a way of synthetically producing cortisone in large quantities at a reasonable cost. Before his discovery, cortisone, used in the treatment of rheumatoid arthritis, was available only in limited quantities and was very expensive.

In the early 1950s, Dr. Julian formed Julian Laboratories, Inc., in Franklin Park, Illinois, and Laboratories Julian de Mexico in Mexico City. In just a few years, Julian Laboratories grew to be one of the largest producers of drugs in the country. In 1961, he sold his Franklin Park Laboratory to the pharmaceutical company of Smith, Kline and French for $2,338,000, but maintained his position as president. During his long and productive career, he received numerous awards, published over 200 papers in respected journals, and had more than 100 patents to his credit.

Dr. Percy Julian died of liver cancer in 1975, but lived to realize his dream; the emergence of Black scientists entering universities, where their creative talents could find uninhibited outlets. Dr. Percy Julian remains a trailblazer for those who have followed him.

ERNEST EVERETT JUST
1883-1941

Ernest Everett Just was recognized as one of this country's most distinguished biological scientists. He formulated new concepts of cell life and metabolism, and pioneered investigations of egg fertilization.

Ernest Just was born August 14, 1883, in Charleston, South Carolina. His father was a dock worker, and his mother was a school teacher. Just's father died when he was only four, and he was forced to start working as a field hand. When he finished high school at 17, Mrs. Just made a courageous and wise decision to send him north for further schooling.

Just managed to graduate from Kimball Union Academy, in New Hampshire, as valedictorian of his class despite the gross racial injustice that he faced. He entered Dartmouth College and received degrees in both history and biology. He was elected to Phi Beta Kappa in his junior year, and was the only student in his class to graduate magna cum laude. It was at Dartmouth that he decided to become a research biologist specializing in cytology, the study of cells.

In 1912, he became head of the biology department at Howard University in Washington, D.C., and held this position until his death. In the meantime, he also became a member of the faculty at the Howard School of Medicine and headed the physiology department. He received a Ph.D. degree in zoology, magna cum laude, from the University of Chicago in 1916.

For 20 years, Dr. Just studied and carried out experiments with the reproductive cells of marine animals at the Marine Biological Laboratory in Cape Cod. He endeavored to contribute to the body of facts, concepts and theories by improving his understanding of cell life. He felt that if we understood the functions of normal and abnormal cells, science would be armed with the knowledge needed to treat many of the ills that plagued humans; such as cancer, leukemia, sickle cell anemia and other diseases involving abnormal cell life.

Dr. Just also blazed new trails in designing techniques for collecting eggs and sperm cells, and laboratory methods of working with the cells. He became an authority of identification procedures to ensure that cells used in experiments were normal, healthy cells. During his lifetime, he authored two books, *Basic Methods for Experiments on Eggs of Marine Animals* and *The Biology of Cell Surface*.

In his book *The Biology of the Cell Surface*, Dr. Just put forth his major theory that the surface of the cell (cell membrane) was as important to the life of a cell as its nucleus. Dr. Just was a contributing editor to various scientific journals, and published more than sixty research papers in leading biological journals.

Dr. Just received many honors for his accomplishments. In 1915, he was the first recipient of the prestigious Spingarn Medal of the NAACP. Although he was never invited to conduct research at any of America's notable laboratories, he was invited to serve as guest researcher at the Kaiser Wilheim Institute of Biology in Germany, the greatest academy of physics, chemistry and biology in the world. He also received similar invitations from the Sorbonne in Paris, and the Zoological Station in Naples, Italy. Dr. Ernest Just died of cancer, at age 58, on October 27, 1941.

There have not been many Americans who have revolutionized man's thinking through science like Dr. Just. He strove hard, not for prizes or world acclaim, but to prove himself as a man in search of the truth through science. In doing so, Dr. Just perhaps has come closer than any other American in revolutionizing our thinking about the nature of living substances.

LEWIS HOWARD LATIMER
1848-1928

Lewis Howard Latimer was a pioneer in the development of the electric light bulb. He was the only Black member of the Edison Pioneers, a group of distinguished scientists and inventors who worked with Thomas Edison.

Latimer, whose father was a former slave, was born in Chelsea, Massachusetts, in 1848, and raised in Boston. At age sixteen, Latimer enlisted in the Navy and served as a cabin boy on the U.S.S. Massasoit for the remainder of the Civil War. In 1865, after receiving an honorable discharge, he returned to Boston seeking work. His skill in mechanical drawing enabled him to secure a position with Crosby and Gould, patent solicitors.

The work of the patent draftsmen fascinated young Latimer, and he taught himself draftsmanship skills. Becoming confident, he asked to be allowed to submit some drawings. The request was begrudgingly granted, but Latimer's impressive work earned him the position of junior draftsman and, in a short time, he was advanced to chief draftsman. During the late 1870s, he married Mary Wilson, and later fathered two daughters.

Around 1876, Alexander Graham Bell recognized his need for a highly skilled draftsman to prepare blueprints for his new invention, the telephone. Bell went to Crosby and Gould, and it was Latimer who was given the assignment to draw the plans for Bell's telephone patent.

In 1879, Latimer left Crosby and Gould to work as a draftsman for Hiram Maxim, who invented the machine gun and also headed the U.S. Electric Lighting Company in Bridgeport, Connecticut. Although electricity was in its infancy, Latimer perceived it to be the wave of the future. Latimer proceeded to work on improving the quality and life of the carbon filament used in the light bulb.

In 1882, Latimer received a patent for what was probably his most important invention, an improved process for manufacturing carbon filaments. This process proved far superior to any other due to longer lasting properties of the elements. The carbon filaments, made from the cellulose of cotton thread or bamboo, were excellent conductors of electricity. He assigned this patent and others to the U.S. Electric Lighting Company.

Latimer left Maxim and transferred to the engineering department at the Edison Company in 1884. He supervised the installation of Edison's electric light systems in New York, Philadelphia, Canada and London. Six years later, Latimer was assigned to the legal department, where he performed an invaluable service as an expert witness, defending Edison's patents in court. Millions of dollars were at stake. Based on Latimer's testimony, Edison won his cases because of Latimer's vast knowledge of electrical patents.

Latimer was a man of many talents and skills, not limited to electrical inventions. Volumes of his love poems were privately published; he also authored a book in 1890, entitled *Incandescent Electric Lighting*.

Lewis Latimer did more than just help to bring electric lights to the streets of New York and its office buildings, homes and subway stations. Through his many activities, he brought "light" to the lives of those around him. He worked for civil rights organizations, and taught recent immigrants mechanical drawing and the English language in a New York City community center.

Lewis Latimer's death, in 1928, was mourned the world over. In honor of his significant contributions to America's industrial revolution, the Lewis H. Latimer Public School, dedicated on May 10, 1968, in Brooklyn, New York, bears his noble name.

FROM THE MINDS OF BLACK INVENTORS:

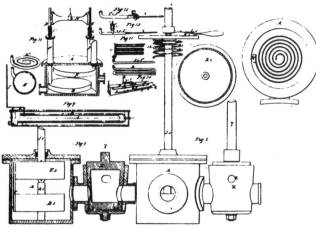

Norbert Rillieux's Sugar Refining Vacuum Pan patented December 10, 1846

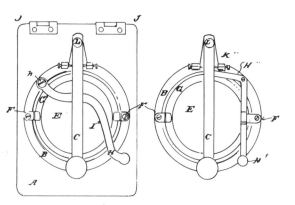

Granville T. Wood's Railway Telegraph patented November 15, 1887

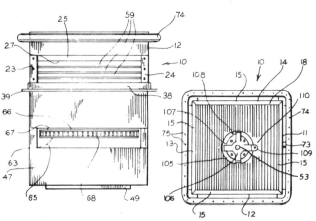

Frederick M. Jones' Air Conditioning Unit patented July 12, 1949

Lewis H. Latimer's Electric La

A. J. Beard's Railroad Co

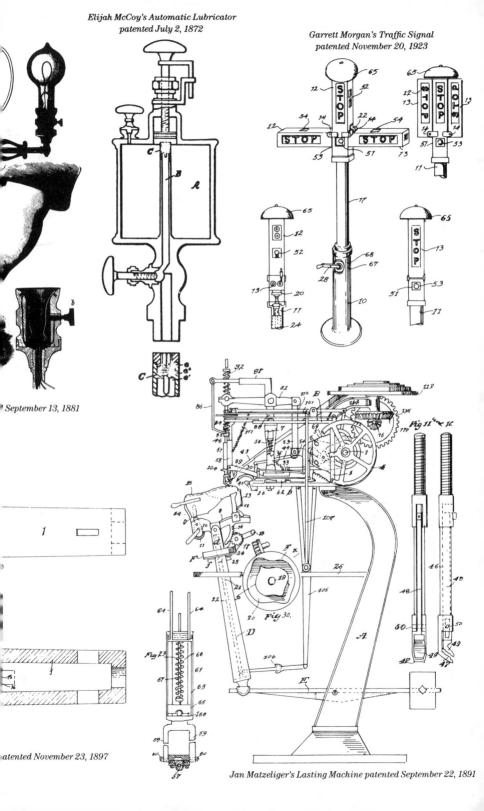

Elijah McCoy's Automatic Lubricator patented July 2, 1872

Garrett Morgan's Traffic Signal patented November 20, 1923

September 13, 1881

atented November 23, 1897

Jan Matzeliger's Lasting Machine patented September 22, 1891

JOSEPH LEE
1849-1905(?)

Stale bread, what to do with it? Joseph Lee can be credited with two inventions in baking technology, the bread crumbing machine and the bread making machine.

As a boy, Joseph Lee's first job was in a bakery were he learned the general business of cooking and the art of making bread. From this boyhood job, he went on to a career of preparing and serving food. He owned two restaurants in Boston, Massachusetts before owning the Woodland Park Hotel in Newton for 17 years.

During the late 1800s, Joseph Lee was bothered by the enormous amount of bread wasted each day because it was a day or so old. He set about to find a way in which to productively make use of stale bread.

Lee, a master cook, knew the superiority of bread crumbs over cracker crumbs. Based on this, he invented and perfected a machine which, by a tearing and grinding process, reduced the bread to crumbs. In his hotel kitchen, these bread crumbs were used in making croquettes, escalloped oysters, dressing for poultry, batter for cakes, puddings, and in frying chops, cutlets, fish, clams and oysters.

On June 4, 1895, the U.S. Patent Office in Washington awarded Patent No. 540,553 to Lee for his bread crumbing machine. He sold his patent rights to a New Hampshire manufacturer, and in a short time it became an essential piece of equipment in every first-class hotel kitchen and restaurant. The Royal Worcester Bread Crumb Co., in Boston, became a lucrative business by manufacturing bread crumbs with Lee's machine.

Joseph Lee didn't stop with the fame and money from his first invention. He went on to invent the first machine for making bread, for which he received a second patent from the U.S. Patent office.

Lee's bread making machine did more than just mix the ingredients. It also kneaded the dough better, cheaper and more hygienically than the bare hands of a baker. Only two or three men were needed to operate the machine, which could produce hundreds of loaves per day. By hand, it took nearly a dozen men to make the same number of loaves each day.

The bread making machine was more than a labor saving device. The kneading done by the machine produced a higher quality of bread that was whiter, finer in texture and softer. In 1902, a pamphlet issued by the National Bread Company, which manufactured Lee's machine, said; "The machine will produce sixty pounds more of finished bread from each barrel of flour."

Also, in 1902, Lee opened the Lee Catering Company on Boylston Street in the Back Bay, where he enjoyed a large, wealthy patronage. During the summer, he took his culinary skills to the South Shore, where he owned and operated the Squantum Inn, a fashionable summer resort, known for its excellent fish dinners.

Joseph Lee was a bread specialist, businessman and restaurateur. His inventive genius in the food industry contributed greatly to the economic and industrial growth of Boston and the country.

JAN EARNST MATZELIGER
1852-1889

Jan Earnst Matzeliger made possible the modernization of the shoe industry by designing and patenting a ("shoe-lasting") machine which would automatically stitch the leather of the shoe to the sole. This in-vention resulted in a lower cost to both the shoe manufacturer and the customer.

Matzeliger was born, in Paramibo, Surinam (Dutch Guiana), in 1852. His mother was a native Black of Surinam, and his father an educated Dutch engineer from a wealthy and aristocratic family in Holland. At age ten, Matzeliger worked as an apprentice in a government machine shop, where his remarkable talent for mechanics surfaced.

At age 19, he signed up on a merchant ship as a seaman for two years. After leaving the ship in Philadelphia, he worked at various odd jobs. A year later, Matzeliger arrived in Lynn, Massachusetts, where he remained for the rest of his life. Lynn was one of the leading shoe manufacturing centers, producing well over half of the nation's shoes. When Matzeliger arrived in Lynn, he could barely speak English.

Matzeliger was able to secure a job with Harney Brothers, a shoe manufacturing factory. He attended evening school and learned to speak English fluently. While working at Harney Brothers as a mechanic, Matzeliger sought to solve a problem that baffled the shoe industry for a long time. Before Matzeliger's invention, the task of attaching the leather uppers to the sole was done by a costly and tedious manual process that required highly skilled craftsmen.

Handlasters were well-paid, but their work was slow and inefficient. As a result, the price of shoes was extremely high. The "last" was a wooden model of the human foot. When a shoemaker judged that the leather had been drawn over the last properly, the edges of the upper leather were tacked to the innersole. The excess leather at the toe was cut and drawn into plaits, which was shaved off to produce a smooth surface when it was attached to the outer sole, usually by sewing. Matzeliger's machine made all of these complex operations more efficient.

In the fall of 1880, Matzeliger constructed a miniature prototype of his shoe lasting machine out of bits of assorted hardware. After six months of hard labor, he produced a larger model. He was offered fifty dollars for his invention, but rejected the offer.

Later, Matzeliger completed an improved model and was offered $1,500, but again he refused. He eventually secured financial backing for his project which enabled him to build a working model. His shoe lasting machine produced shoes ten times faster than the skilled hands of a shoe craftsman.

Matzeliger's invention made Lynn, Massachusetts "the undisputed shoe capital of the world." Over the next two years, he obtained four more patents on specific improvements on his shoe lasting machine. By 1889, the demand for the new "head laster" had become worldwide. The companies that emerged, from the fruits of his labor, formed the United Shoe Machinery Corporation and, by 1955, had holdings of over a billion dollars.

In 1886, Matzeliger caught a cold which developed into tuberculosis. He died in August, 1889, at the age of 37. On May 16, 1967, the City of Lynn, Massachusetts honored its 19th century inventor. Sponsored by the local branch of the NAACP, May 16th was declared Jan E. Matzeliger Day. Today, in shoe manufacturing centers, machinery very similar to the Jan Matzeliger original is still in use.

ELIJAH J. McCOY
1843-1929

Elijah McCoy was a mechanical engineer and the inventor of a revolutionary device, which made it possible to lubricate the moving parts of a machine, while it was operating.

Elijah McCoy was born in Colchester, Ontario, Canada, in 1843. His parents, George and Mildred McCoy, had escaped as slaves from Kentucky and fled to Canada, by way of the Underground Railroad. McCoy's father labored endlessly to send his son abroad to obtain a good education. At age 15, young McCoy went to Edinburgh, Scotland to study. Upon completion of his studies in Scotland, he returned to the United States well-trained and eager to begin his career in engineering.

Although his credentials were extraordinary, McCoy was repeatedly denied a position in engineering because of his race. Finally, accepting a job as a fireman for the Michigan Central Railroad, he had the menial task of shoveling coal into the engine and oiling all of the train's moving parts. Bored with this procedure, he asked himself, "Why can't this train lubricate itself?" This question prompted McCoy to begin experimenting with a mechanical self-lubricating device.

In 1870, McCoy gained instant fame in the field of mechanical engineering. He started the Elijah McCoy Manufacturing Company in Detroit, Michigan. In this shop, he invented the first automatic lubricator, called the "lubricator cup," and was granted a United States patent on July 2, 1872. His device allowed small amounts of oil to drip continuously onto the moving parts of a machine while it was in operation.

Prior to McCoy's invention, all motorized machinery had to be periodically brought to a complete stop so lubricants could be applied by hand. McCoy's lubricator cup became an extremely important invention to industry because it reduced time and labor costs significantly, and increased business profits substantially.

In time, anyone who owned a self-lubricating machine bragged of having the "real McCoy," an expression that is still used today to signify genuine quality. McCoy soon improved upon this first model with more sophisticated ones. For the next twenty-five years, he made various changes and patented more than fifty different automatic lubricators. Later, he specialized in lubricating devices for special kinds of machinery such as air brakes and steam engines.

Invitations soon started to pour in from large industries, here and abroad, asking McCoy to serve as a consultant or lecturer. Although major industrialists requested his services and expertise in the field, many were not aware of his race. They were often quite surprised to learn that this ingenious invention was conceived by a Black man. There were times when they would cancel McCoy's scheduled appearances because of racial prejudice, some even refused to use the lubricator they so badly needed.

Elijah McCoy died in Detroit, Michigan at age 85, in 1929. "The real McCoy" process is still employed in our modern day machinery such as automobiles, locomotives, rockets, ships, and a vast number of other machines. McCoy's invention will always be remembered for modernizing the industrial world.

GARRETT A. MORGAN
1875-1963

Garrett A. Morgan is best remembered for his invention of the automatic traffic signal, which brought order from chaos in the nation's streets and improved traffic safety. He also invented a gas mask, widely used by firemen in American cities in the early 1900s, and by soldiers on the battlefields of Europe during World War I.

Garrett was born March 4, 1875, in Paris, Kentucky, the seventh of eleven children born to Elizabeth and Sydney Morgan. He left school after the fifth grade, at the age of 14. Leaving Kentucky and heading for Cincinnati, Ohio, he secured a job as a handy man in a sewing machine shop.

Morgan's first invention was a belt fastener for sewing machines, which he sold, in 1901, for $50.00. In 1909, he opened a tailoring shop, employing 32 workers, which manufactured dresses, suits and coats. After only one year in business, he was able to buy a home for his wife, Mary Anne Hassek. They later had three sons.

In 1913, Morgan inadvertently discovered a substance that would straighten hair, which he later marketed. The business profits, reaped from the G. A. Morgan Hair Refining Company, enabled Morgan to concentrate on his other inventions.

Morgan directed his attention to the frequent instances of firemen being overcome by fumes and thick smoke when they entered burning buildings. Many respiratory devices of that time were not dependable and frequently malfunctioned. Consequently, Morgan perfected a breathing device which he patented in 1914.

This gas mask was widely used by engineers, chemists and working men who were exposed to noxious fumes or dust. He later modified it to carry its own air supply, and it had great significance on World War I battlefields and in subsequent wars. Morgan founded the National Safety Device Company and extensively utilized the advertising media to promote his invention.

On the night of July 25, 1916, a tunnel being constructed under Lake Erie exploded, leaving many workers of the Cleveland Water Works trapped, and some died in the "death tunnel." Morgan and his brother Frank were summoned. Wearing gas masks, Morgan, Frank and two volunteers courageously entered the tunnel because fire and police officials were afraid to do so. They all emerged safely, and many lives were saved. Morgan's heroic feat appeared in newspapers all over the country. He was awarded medals from the International Association of Fire Engineers, which made him an honorary member of the Cleveland Citizens' Group. He received a solid gold medal and the grand prize at the Second International Exposition of Safety and Sanitation.

In 1923, Morgan patented an automatic traffic signal. This signal became the forerunner of the overhead and sidewalk traffic lights that we use each day. He sold this invention to the General Electric Company for $4,000.

In the 1920s, Morgan embarked upon a completely different endeavor. He and his colleagues started a newspaper, the *Cleveland Call,* now the *Cleveland Call and Post,* which has one of the largest circulations of any Black newspaper in the Midwest today.

In 1963, Garrett A. Morgan died at the age of 88, in Cleveland, Ohio, after two years of illness. Through his creative mind and astute business skills, the world is a safer and more orderly place in which to live.

NORBERT RILLIEUX
1806-1894

Norbert Rillieux is credited for stopping the "Jamaica Train" (a crude sugar refining process) dead in its tracks, even though it was not associated with any railroad. Rillieux's invention was responsible for simplifying and improving the process of refining sugar.

He was born a mulatto, free man in New Orleans, in 1806. His mother was a slave and his father a successful, wealthy White engineer who invented a steam-operated cotton bailing press.

Rillieux received his education in the New Orleans' Catholic school system. However, due to discrimination and the unavailability of advanced schooling, he was sent to Paris to study at the L'Ecole Centrale. At the age of 24, he became an instructor of applied mechanics at L'Ecole Centrale, publishing a series of papers on the steam engine and steam economy.

Rillieux's strong interest in his father's plantation, coupled with his theory on multiple effect evaporation, provided the basis for his famous invention. The "Jamaica Train," a slow, expensive and hazardous sugar production process, was what he set out to improve upon. Rillieux's invention was a significant one. His refining method was a series of vacuum pans combined to make the heated vapor evaporate sugar, pan-by-pan, into crystallized granules. Before his invention, sugar was a luxury item and used only on special occasions.

Rillieux's invention has been hailed as one of the greatest in the history of chemical engineering. It resulted in saving fuel, manpower and time, giving the United States worldwide sugar industry supremacy. Nonetheless, Rillieux never received recognition in any chemistry, physics or technical journals.

Rillieux's invention did not come without its trials. He attempted to devise his evaporation process in 1834 and failed. In 1841, he tried again and failed. Doubting the worth of his invention, he became discouraged, and it was not until 1843 that he succeeded in obtaining a patent.

In 1846, Rillieux received yet another patent for an improvement on his evaporator design. Today, the process of multiple effect, with little change from Rillieux's basic principle, is universally used for the manufacturing of sugar, condensed milk, soap, gelatin and glue. His method is also employed in the recovery of waste liquids in distilleries and factories.

Another Rillieux invention was an engineering plan to rid New Orleans' sewage system of its yellow-fever infested mosquitos. Yellow fever claimed the lives of many New Orleans citizens. Rillieux submitted his plan to city authorities, but they refused to use it. The authorities later accepted a similar plan submitted by a group of Whites. After refusing to endure any more racial and professional prejudices, Rillieux returned to France in 1854, becoming headmaster at his alma mater L'Ecole Centrale.

Lack of recognition troubled Rillieux throughout his life. He died in October, 1894, at the age of 88, and was buried in the churchyard of the Pere La Chaise Cemetery in Paris. Thirty years after his death, a movement to honor Rillieux began in Holland, and quickly spread to every sugar producing country in the world. In 1934, after much delay and evasion, New Orleans honored Rillieux with a plaque in the Louisiana State Museum.

LEWIS TEMPLE
1800-1854

Lewis Temple was the inventor of a whaling harpoon, known as "Temple's Toggle" and "Temple's Iron," that became the standard harpoon of the whaling industry in the middle of the 19th century.

Lewis Temple was a skilled blacksmith. He was not a whaler and had never gone to sea. Temple was born a slave in Richmond, Virginia, in 1800, and arrived in New Bedford, Massachusetts in 1829. By 1836, Temple was one of the 315,000 free Black people in the United States, and a successful businessman who operated a whalecraft shop on the New Bedford waterfront.

By 1836, Temple, a well-known citizen of New Bedford, and working as a blacksmith to support his wife, Mary Clark, whom he married in 1829, and their three children. In 1845, Temple was able to open a larger shop.

The procuring of whale oil, whale meat and other by-products was a leading industry in Massachusetts and New England. Whaling also provided thousands of jobs for seamen, many of whom were Black. Based on conversations with the whalers who came to his shop to have their whaling tools made and to buy harpoons, Temple learned that many whales escaped, since the harpoons used at the time were not particularly effective in holding a struggling whale.

In 1848, Lewis Temple invented a new type of harpoon, with a movable head, that prevented the whale from slipping loose. The Temple Iron was more effective than any other harpoon that had ever been manufactured. The head on Temple's harpoon became locked in the whale's flesh, and the only way to free the harpoon was to cut it loose after the whale was killed.

Initially, whalers did not accept Temple's harpoon. However, after some trials, most whaling captains were convinced that Temple's "Toggle-Iron" was far superior to the ordinary barbed head harpoon. Lewis Temple never patented his invention, but was able to make a fairly good living from his harpoon sales. This sum, of course, was nowhere near the fortune he could have made, if he had patented his invention. Temple was able to buy the building next to his shop and, in 1854, arranged for construction of a blacksmith shop near Steamboat Wharf.

Temple accidentally fell one night, while walking near his new shop's construction site. He never fully recovered from his injuries. Temple was unable to return to work and money became scarce for his family. He died destitute in May, 1854, at the age of 54. When his estate was settled, practically everything he owned was used to pay off his debts.

Clifford W. Ashley, an authority on the history of whaling, said in his book, *The Yankee Whaler*, that Temple's harpoon was "the single most important invention in the whole history of whaling."

GRANVILLE T. WOODS
1856-1910

Granville T. Woods, known as the "Black Edison," was an extremely prolific and brilliant inventor of electro-mechanical devices. His inventions produced broader and more efficient applications of electricity. Woods' early genius for modifying and improving electrical apparatus was unsurpassed during America's Industrial Revolution.

A native of Columbus, Ohio, Granville attended school until the age of 10. At age 16, he traveled to Missouri and worked as a fireman-engineer on the railroads. Afterwards, he traveled east to study electrical and mechanical engineering, and was able to obtain a job on a British steamer, the *Ironside*, where he remained for two years.

By 1881, Woods opened a factory in Cincinnati, Ohio and manufactured telephone, telegraph and electrical equipment. He filed his first application for a patent in 1884, for an improved steam boiler furnace. Later that same year, he invented a telephone transmitter. His transmitter could carry the voice over longer distances, with greater clarity and more distinct sound.

A year later, Woods patented an apparatus he coined the "telegraphony," a combination of the telephone and telegraph. As a result, telegraph stations could send both oral and signal messages over the same line. An inexperienced telegraph operator could now send messages without benefit of knowing the Morse code. Woods sold this invention to the American Bell Telephone Company.

Woods produced one of his most important inventions in 1887: a device called the Synchronous Multiplex Railway Telegraph. It enabled messages to be sent to and from moving trains and railway stations. Serious accidents were avoided because conductors could be forewarned of obstacles in their path. Another key invention of Woods was a regulator, which greatly increased the efficiency of electric motors. Demands for his electrical devices became so widespread that he abandoned his company to devote full-time to further inventions.

After relocating to New York City, in 1890, Woods became a patron of the arts. It was while attending the theater that he became fascinated by the way theater lights were gradually "dimmed." However, this dimming system was known to cause electrical fires, so he set out to improve this lighting system by creating an efficient, safe and economical dimmer. His system was not only safer, but resulted in a 40% energy savings.

Woods was also responsible for modernizing our transportation system. He invented an overhead conducting system for electric railways, still utilized by trains and trolley cars today. He also invented the electrified "third rail," now used by subway systems in large cities such as Chicago, New York and elsewhere. In 1901, this invention was sold to the General Electric Company in New York.

Granville T. Woods was awarded more than 35 patents for his electrical innovations. In 1890, he introduced an electrically heated egg incubator, which made it possible to hatch 50,000 eggs at one time. He also invented a relay instrument, an electro mechanical brake, a galvanic battery, an automatic safety cutout for electrical circuits, and many other devices.

At the time of his death in 1910, more than 150 patents had been awarded to Granville Woods. His achievements attracted universal attention and high praise from the scientific community worldwide.

LOUIS TOMPKINS WRIGHT
1891-1952

Louis Tompkins Wright, a pioneer in clinical antibiotic research, was the first Black physician to be appointed to the staff of a New York municipal hospital; the first Black physician in America to head a public interracial hospital; and the second Black surgeon to be admitted to the American College of Surgeons (1931).

Born in LaGrange, Georgia, July 23, 1891, Louis was the youngest of two sons of Dr. Ceah and Lula Wright. His Father graduated from Meharry Medical College in 1881. Wright's father died and, four years later, his mother married Dr. William Fletcher Penn, the first Black to graduate from Yale Medical School in 1898. Dr. Penn inspired Wright to study medicine.

Wright was valedictorian of his class in 1911, at Clark College in Atlanta, Georgia. After graduation, he applied for admission to Harvard Medical School, and was told he would be admitted if he could pass an exam in chemistry. He accepted the challenge and passed the exam with flying colors. He graduated cum laude in 1915, fourth in his class. In spite of graduating with honors from Harvard Medical School, he was not given an internship at any White hospital because of his race. He completed his internship at Freeman's Hospital in Washington D.C.

In 1917, Dr. Wright enlisted in the United States Army as a first lieutenant in the Medical Corps. While there, he introduced the intradermal method of vaccination for smallpox. His new method eliminated previously encountered side effects. He was later placed in charge of a military hospital in France, becoming the youngest surgeon to be given such a position. In France, he suffered permanent lung damage from a poisonous gas attack. When the war ended, he was awarded the Purple

Heart and discharged at the rank of captain. He subsequen rose to the rank of lieutenant colonel in the reserves.

In 1918, he married Corinne Cooke. They had two daug ters, who became doctors. One daughter became the first Blac woman to be dean of a New York medical college. In 1919, D Wright became the first Black surgeon to be appointed to th wealthy White Harlem Hospital in New York. Four Whit doctors resigned in protest of his appointment. He went on t become the director of surgery, and later president of the Harlem Medical Board.

Dr. Wright became an authority in the area of head injuries, and was asked to write a chapter in the eleventh edition of Schudder's Treatment of Fractures. He devised a brace for fractures of the neck that is still in use today, and he also invented a special blade plate for surgical treatment on fractures of the knee joint.

Beyond his surgical specialty, Dr. Wright became an authority on the use of aureomycin, an antibiotic, becoming the first in the world to experiment with this new drug on humans with success. In all, he had 89 scientific publications to his credit, including his publications on chemotherapy in the treatment of cancer.

A conscientious crusader for the equal rights of Blacks, he led a constant and unflinching battle against racial injustice. He held the American Medical Association responsible for racial discrimination in medical care, and publicly stated that "the American Medical Association has demonstrated as much interest in the health of the Negro as Hitler has in the health of the Jew. Someday the nation will wake up to the fact that disease germs are not color conscious."

Dr. Louis Tompkins Wright suffered a heart attack and died, at age sixty-one, in October, 1952. It has been stated that he was one of the "most productive, and most distinguished Black physicians to appear on the American scene."

TEST YOURSELF

Now that you have familiarized yourself with our historic Black scientists and inventors in this second series of Empak's Black History publications, this section, in three parts: MATCH; TRUE/FALSE; MULTIPLE CHOICE/FILL-IN, is designed to help you remember some key points about each notable Black scientist and inventor. (Answers on page 28)

MATCH

I. *Match the column on the right with the column on the left by placing the appropriate alphabetical letter next to the scientist or inventor it represents.*

1. Andrew J. Beard_____
2. Granville T. Woods_____
3. Percy L. Julian_____
4. Elijah McCoy_____
5. Norbert Rillieux_____
6. Garrett A. Morgan_____
7. Frederick M. Jones_____

A) Authenticity
B) Gas Mask
C) The Jamaica Train
D) Jenny Coupler
E) Soybean Chemist
F) The Black Edison
G) Toggle Iron
H) Refrigeration Unit

TRUE/FALSE

II. *The True and False statements below are taken from the biographical information given on each of the scientist and inventors.*

1. Lewis Temple, inventor of the Toggle harpoon, spent long, tedious voyages in search of whales._____
2. Joseph Lee invented a device which was associated with the railroad and saved many lives and countless maimings. _____
3. Dr. Lloyd A. Hall was a noted food chemist. He developed a salt formula to protect foods containing fats and oils from spoilage and rancidity. _____
4. Lewis Latimer supervised the installation of electric light plants in the U.S. and Europe. _____
5. James Forten invented a device that made it easier to handle the sails of large ships. _____
6. Jan Matzeliger is responsible for inventing the "third rail" track used by present-day subway trains. _____
7. Dr. Ernest Just, a distinguished biological scientist, initiated pioneer investigations of egg fertilization. _____

MULTIPLE CHOICE/FILL-IN

III. *Complete the statements below by drawing a line under the correct name, or by filling-in the correct answer which you have read in the biographical sketches.*

1. _____ developed the theory of multiple effect evaporation which revolutionized the sugar industry.
2. The noted scientist and surgeon who first experimented successfully, on humans, with the antibiotic aureomycin was (Dr. E. Just, Dr. Louis T. Wright, Dr. Lloyd A. Hall).
3. _____ invented two pioneering machines which were the forerunners of today's baking technology.
4. The self-taught mathematician and astronomer (Frederick M. Jones, Garrett A. Morgan, Benjamin Banneker) who built the first American-made clock, is also credited with producing the building plans of Washington, D.C., the nation's capital.
5. The agricultural genius,_____ , discovered hundreds of uses from peanuts, sweet potatoes, soybeans, pecans, and clay, and revolutionized the dying economy of the South.
6. The world authority on the preservation of blood was (Dr. Charles R. Drew, Dr. Lloyd A. Hall, Dr. Percy L. Julian). He organized the world's first mass blood bank for Great Britain and also established the American Red Cross Blood Bank.
7. _____ invented a shoe lasting machine which revolutionized the shoe industry and made Lynn, Massachusetts the "Shoe Capital of the World".

ACROSS

1. Father time
4. Forged a whale of an iron
7. Banked the substance of life
9. Smooth Sailing
10. Out "lasted" the best of them
13. Formulated new concepts of cell life
14. Stop & Go
16. Coined telelgraphony

DOWN

1. A close connection of a rail kind
2. One lump or two
3. The nut cracker
5. Little dough boy
6. Slippery when oiled
8. Antibiotic researcher
9. For want of a cool breeze
11. Illuminated the world
12. A sight for sore eyes
15. Pass the salt, please

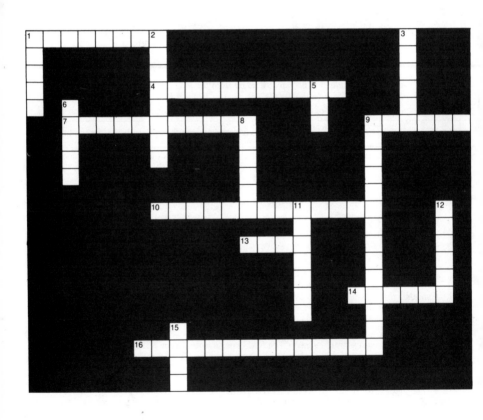

WORDSEARCH

1. Benjamin Banneker
2. Andrew Beard
3. George Washington Carver
4. Charles Drew
5. James Forten
6. Lloyd Hall

7. Frederick Jones
8. Percy Julian
9. Ernest Just
10. Lewis Latimer
11. Joseph Lee
12. Jan Matzeliger

13. Elijah McCoy
14. Garrett Morgan
15. Norbert Rillieux
16. Lewis Temple
17. Granville Woods
18. Louis Wright

The names of our eighteen HISTORIC BLACK SCIENTISTS AND INVENTORS are contained in the diagram below. Look in the diagram of letters for the names given in the list. Find the names by reading FORWARD, BACKWARDS, UP, DOWN, and DIAGONALLY in a straight line of letters. Each time you find a name in the diagram, circle it in the diagram and cross it off on the list of names. Words often overlap, and letters may be used more than once.

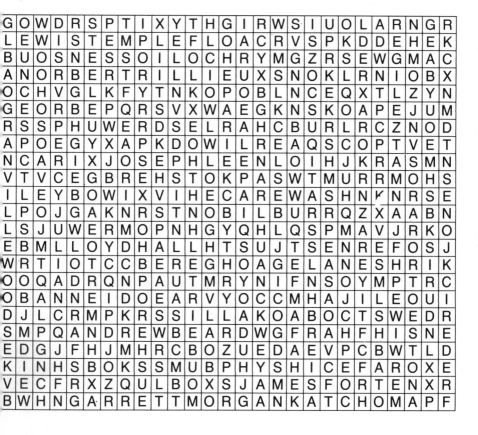

MATCH

1.–D	5.–C
2.–F	6.–B
3.–E	7.–H
4.–A	

TRUE/FALSE

1.–FALSE	5.–TRUE
2.–FALSE	6.–FALSE
3.–TRUE	7.–TRUE
4.–TRUE	

MULTIPLE CHOICE/FILL IN

1. NORBERT RILLIEUX
2. DR. LOUIS T. WRIGHT
3. JOSEPH LEE
4. BENJAMIN BANNEKER

5. GEORGE WASHINGTON CARVER
6. DR. CHARLES DREW
7. JAN E. MATZELIGER

CROSSWORD PUZZLE

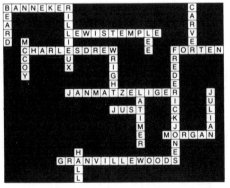

WORD SEARCH

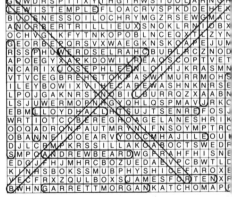

Send to: Empak Publishing Company, 212 E. Ohio St., Suite 300, Chicago, IL 60611—Phone: (312) 642-8364

Name _____

Affiliation _____

Address _____
P. O. Box numbers not accepted, street address must appear.

City _____ State _____ Zip _____

Phone# (_____)_____ Date _____

Method Of Payment Enclosed:　　( ) Check　　　　( ) Money Order　　　　( ) Purchase Order

Prices effective 11/1/95 thru 10/31/96

ADVANCED LEVEL

Quantity	ISBN #	Title Description	Unit Price	Total Price
	0-922162-1-8	"A Salute to Historic Black Women"		
	0-922162-2-6	"A Salute to Black Scientists & Inventors"		
	0-922162-3-4	"A Salute to Black Pioneers"		
	0-922162-4-2	"A Salute to Black Civil Rights Leaders"		
	0-922162-5-0	"A Salute to Historic Black Abolitionists"		
	0-922162-6-9	"A Salute to Historic African Kings & Queens"		
	0-922162-7-7	"A Salute to Historic Black Firsts"		
	0-922162-8-5	"A Salute to Historic Blacks in the Arts"		
	0-922162-9-3	"A Salute to Blacks in the Federal Government"		
	0-922162-14-X	"A Salute to Historic Black Educators"		

INTERMEDIATE LEVEL

	0-922162-75-1	"Historic Black Women"		
	0-922162-76-X	"Black Scientists & Inventors"		
	0-922162-77-8	"Historic Black Pioneers"		
	0-922162-78-6	"Black Civil Rights Leaders"		
	0-922162-80-8	"Historic Black Abolitionists"		
	0-922162-81-6	"Historic African Kings & Queens"		
	0-922162-82-4	"Historic Black Firsts"		
	0-922162-83-2	"Historic Blacks in the Arts"		
	0-922162-84-0	"Blacks in the Federal Government"		
	0-922162-85-9	"Historic Black Educators"		

Total Books	❸ Subtotal	
	❹ IL Residents add 8.75% Sales Tax	
SEE ABOVE CHART ▷	❺ Shipping & Handling	
GRADE LEVEL: 4th, 5th, 6th	❻ Total	

BOOK PRICING ● QUANTITY DISCOUNTS

Advanced Level	Intermediate Level
Reg. $3.49	Reg. $2.29
Order 50 or More	Order 50 or More
Save 40¢ EACH	Save 20¢ EACH
@ $3.09	@ $2.09

❺ SHIPPING AND HANDLING

Order Total	Add
Under $5.00	$1.50
$5.01-$15.00	$3.00
$15.01-$35.00	$4.50
$35.01-$75.00	$7.00
$75.01-$200.00	10%
Over $201.00	6%

In addition to the above charges, U.S. territories, HI & AK, add $2.00. Canada & Mexico, add $5.00. Other outside U.S., add $20.00.

Name_____

Affiliation_____

Street_____
P. O. Box numbers not accepted, street address must appear.

City_____State _____ Zip _____

Phone (_____)_____ Date _____

Method Of Payment Enclosed: ( ) Check   ( ) Money Order   ( ) Purchase Order

Prices effective 11/1/95 thru 10/31/96

PRIMARY LEVEL... KINDERGARTEN, FIRST, SECOND & THIRD GRADE

Quantity	ISBN #	Title Description	Unit Price	Total Price
	0-922162-90-5	"Kumi and Chanti"		
	0-922162-91-3	"George Washington Carver"		
	0-922162-92-1	"Harriet Tubman"		
	0-922162-93-X	"Jean Baptist DuSable"		
	0-922162-94-8	"Matthew Henson"		
	0-922162-95-6	"Bessie Coleman"		
Total Books			❸ Subtotal	
			❹ IL Residents add 8.75% Sales Tax	
	SEE CHART BELOW ▷		❺ Shipping & Handling	
			❻ Total	

KEY STEPS IN ORDERING
❶ Establish quantity needs.   ❹ Add tax, if applicable.
❷ Determine book unit price.   ❺ Add shipping &handling.
❸ Determine total cost.   ❻ Total amount.

BOOK PRICING ● QUANTITY DISCOUNTS

❶ Quantity Ordered	❷ Unit Price
1-49	$3.49
50 +	$3.09

❺ SHIPPING AND HANDLING

Order Total	Add
Under $5	$1.50
$5.01-$15.00	$3.00
$15.01- $35.00	$4.50
$35.01-$75.00	$7.00
$75.01-$200.00	10%
Over $201.00	6%

In addition to the above charges, U.S. territories, HI & AK, add $2.00. Canada and Mexico, add $5.00. Other outside U.S., add $20.00.

Empak Publishing provides attractive counter and floor displays for retailers and organizations interested in the Heritage book series for resale. Please check here ☐ and include this form with your letterhead and we will send you specific information and our special volume discounts.

- The Empak "Heritage Kids" series provides a basic understanding and appreciation of Black history which translates to cultural awareness, self-esteem, and ethnic pride within young African-American children.

- Assisted by dynamic and impressive 4-color illustrations, readers will be able to relate to the two adorable African kids -- Kumi & Chanti, as they are introduced to the inspirational lives and deeds of significant, historic African-Americans.

Black History Materials
Available from Empak Publishing

A Salute To Black History Poster Series
African-American Experience–Period Poster Series
Biographical Poster Series
Heritage Kids Poster Series

Advanced Booklet Series
Instructor's Manuals
Advanced Skills Sheets
Black History Bulletin Board Aids
Instructor's Kits

Intermediate Booklet Series
Teacher's Guides
Intermediate Skill Sheets
Black History Flashcards
Intermediate Reading Certificates
Teacher's Kits

Heritage Kids Booklet Series
Heritage Kids Resource & Activity Guides
Heritage Kids Reading Certificates
Heritage Kids Kits

Black History Videos
Black History Month Activity & Resource Guide
African-American Times–A Chronological Record
African-American Discovery Board Game
African-American Clip Art
Black History Mugs
Black Heritage Marble Engraving
Black History Month Banners (18" x 60")
Say YES to Black History Education Sweatshirts
Say YES to Black History Education T-Shirts

To receive your copy of the Empak Publishing Company's
colorful new catalog, please send $2 to cover postage and handling to:

Empak Publishing Company
Catalog Dept., Suite 300
212 East Ohio Street
Chicago, IL 60611